I0803714

EXPLORING COUNTRIES

SOUTH AFRICA

Tracy Vonder Brink

TABLE OF CONTENTS

A Crabtree Seedlings Book

Crabtree Publishing
crabtreebooks.com

School-to-Home Support for Caregivers and Teachers

This book helps children grow by letting them practice reading. Here are a few guiding questions to help the reader with building his or her comprehension skills. Possible answers appear here in red.

Before Reading:

- What do I think this book is about?
    - *I think this book is about South Africa.*
    - *I think this book is about the people of South Africa.*
- What do I want to learn about this topic?
    - *I want to learn where South Africa is.*
    - *I want to learn about some of South Africa's cities.*

During Reading:

- I wonder why...
    - *I wonder why South Africa has three capitals.*
    - *I wonder why South Africa has so many animals.*
- What have I learned so far?
    - *I have learned that the Orange River is the longest river in South Africa.*
    - *I have learned that grasslands cover much of South Africa.*

After Reading:

- What details did I learn about this topic?
    - *I have learned that Namaqualand is a desert that is sometimes filled with flowers.*
    - *I have learned that zebras live in South Africa.*
- Read the book again and look for the vocabulary words.
    - *I see the word* ***capital*** *on page 4, and the word* ***desert*** *on page 18. The other glossary words are on pages 22 and 23.*

South Africa is a country.

It is in **Africa**.

South Africa has three **capital** cities.

Pretoria is the main capital.

The president of South Africa lives and works there.

South Africa has 11 official languages. Many people speak IsiZulu.

Cape Town is the capital city where the **government** makes laws.

More than 4 million people live in Cape Town.

Bloemfontein is the **judicial** capital of South Africa.

The Atlantic Ocean is on one side of South Africa.

The Indian Ocean is on the other side.

Sharks hunt along South Africa's **coast**.

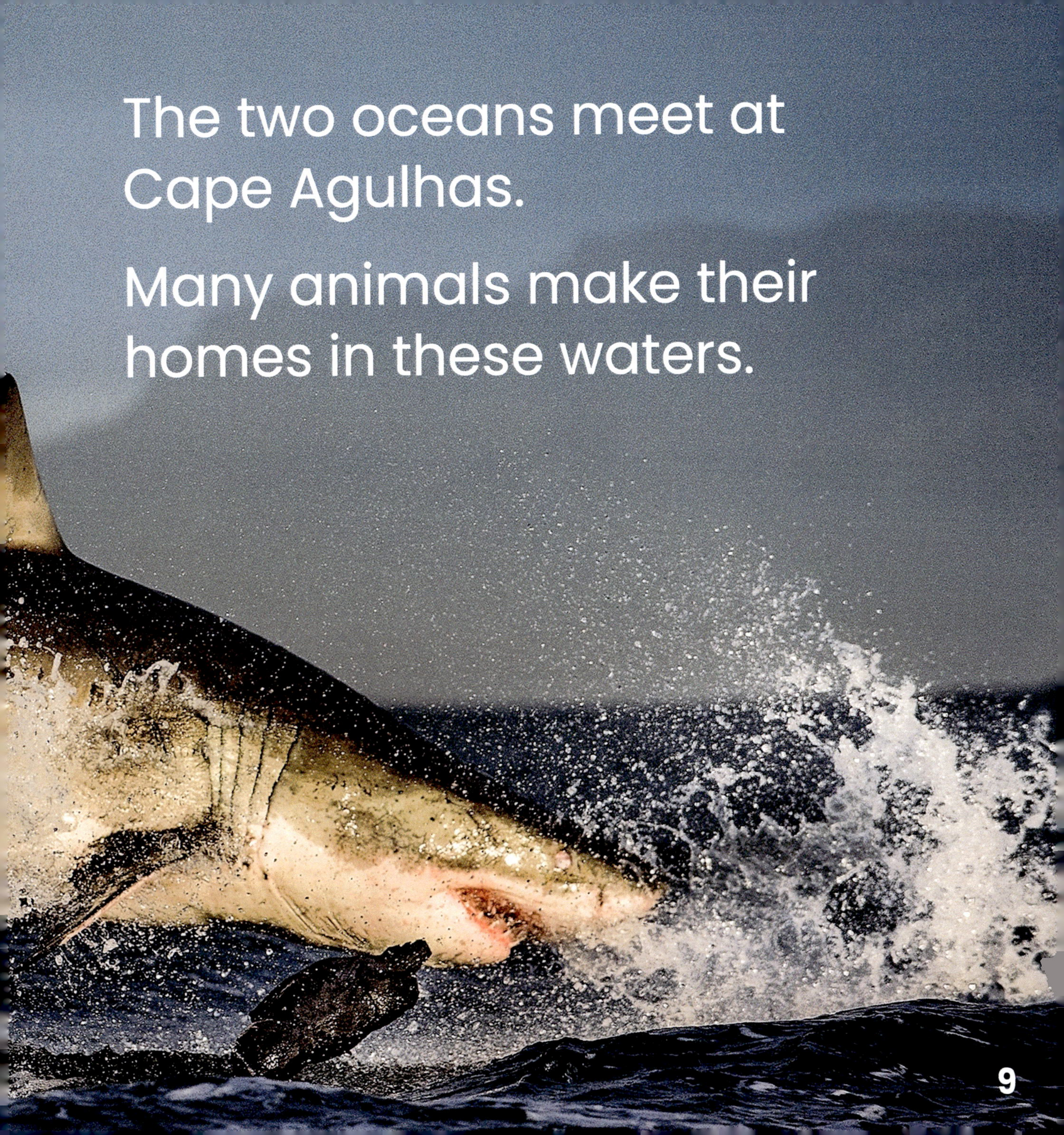

The two oceans meet at Cape Agulhas.

Many animals make their homes in these waters.

Grasslands cover much of South Africa.

Zebras live there.

The Drakensberg is South Africa's longest mountain range.

Its name means Dragon Mountains.

The Orange River starts in the Drakensberg.

The Orange River is the longest river in South Africa.

It flows to Augrabies Falls.

The Cape Floral Kingdom is on the coast.

About 9,000 different kinds of plants grow there.

Namaqualand is a **desert**.

But sometimes it is filled with flowers.

Daisies bloom after the spring rain.

South Africa has **unique** animals.

Elephants, lions, rhinos, and leopards all live there.

South Africa has many things to see!

Glossary

Africa (AF-ri-kuh): The continent south of Europe and between the Indian and Atlantic Oceans

capital (KAP-i-tl): The city where the government of a country or a state is located

coast (kohst): The land next to the ocean or sea

desert (DEH-zert): A very dry area that gets a small amount of rain per year

government (GUHV-ern-muhnt): The group of people who make decisions for a country

judicial (joo-DISH-uhl): Relating to judges or courts of law

unique (yoo-NEEK): Very special and unlike anything else

Index

About the Author

Tracy Vonder Brink

Tracy Vonder Brink loves to visit new places. She has never visited South Africa but wishes she could see a lion. She lives in Cincinnati, Ohio, with her husband, two daughters, and two rescue dogs.

Written by: Tracy Vonder Brink
Designed by: Rhea Magaro
Series Development: James Earley
Proofreader: Melissa Boyce
Educational Consultant: Marie Lemke M.Ed.

Photographs: All images from Shutterstock

Crabtree Publishing

crabtreebooks.com 800-387-7650

Printed in the U.S.A./062024/CG20240201

Published in Canada
Crabtree Publishing
616 Welland Avenue
St. Catharines, Ontario
L2M 5V6

Published in the United States
Crabtree Publishing
347 Fifth Avenue
Suite 1402-145
New York, New York, 10016

Library and Archives Canada Cataloguing in Publication
Available at Library and Archives Canada

Library of Congress Cataloging-in-Publication Data
Available at the Library of Congress

Hardcover: 978-1-0398-4482-7
Paperback: 978-1-0398-4563-3
Ebook (pdf): 978-1-0398-4635-7
Epub: 978-1-0398-4705-7
Read-Along: 978-1-0398-4775-0
Audio: 978-1-0398-4845-0